# GUIDELINES FOR BIBLIOGRAPHIC DESCRIPTION OF REPRODUCTIONS

Committee on Cataloging: Description and Access
Cataloging and Classification Section
Association for Library Collections & Technical Services

Bruce Chr. Johnson, Principal Editor

American Library Association
Chicago and London
1995

Acquiring editor: Arthur Plotnik

Project manager: David M. Epstein

Cover design: Richmond Jones

Composition by Dianne M. Rooney in Times using
QuarkXpress 3.3 for the Mac 7100/66

Printed on 50-pound Husky Smooth, a pH-neutral stock,
and bound in 10-point C1S cover stock by Commercial
Communications, Inc.

The paper used in this publication meets the minimum
requirements of American National Standard for Information
Sciences—Permanence of Paper for Printed Library
Materials, ANSI Z39. 48-1992. ∞

ISBN: 0-8389-3450-1

Printed in the United States of America

99  98  97  96  95        5  4  3  2  1

# CONTENTS

# WITHDRAWN

# FOREWORD

The *Guidelines for Bibliographic Description of Reproductions* have as their starting point the discussions of the Library of Congress Multiple Versions Committee. This committee, meeting in the late 1980s, tried to identify a satisfactory method for bringing together disparate manifestations of otherwise identical library materials. The opening sentences of their discussion paper, *Communication of Records for Multiple Versions,* dated April 21, 1988, stated:

> Multiple versions, i.e., items having identical content and appearing in different physical formats, present problems in cataloging, in retrieval, and in interpretation of the catalog. The purpose of this paper is to promote discussion about the communication of USMARC records for multiple versions. It is, consequently, subject to change. It is anticipated that several parties will want to review and discuss these matters and we look forward to hearing their comments.

Two early MARBI (Machine-Readable Bibliographic Information Committee) discussion papers (numbers twenty-one and twenty-five) on multiple versions, were widely distributed and received the attention of the American Library Association's Committee on Cataloging: Description and Access (CC:DA). It was clear from the earliest discussions that defining what was meant by multiple versions and then determining how to frame guidelines for cataloging them would be very difficult.

The Library of Congress organized a Multiple Versions Forum on December 5–7, 1989, at the Airlie House in Warrenton, Virginia. This gathering, which came to be referred to as the "Airlie House Forum," discussed in great detail what was meant by *multiple versions,* and how they should be handled in the context of the *Anglo-American Cataloguing Rules,* second edition, 1988 revision (AACR2R) and the USMARC bibliographic format. While the Airlie House Forum was able to reach several conclusions about multiple versions, the Forum asked CC:DA to develop descriptive cataloging guidelines for carrying out these conclusions.

The *Guidelines for Bibliographic Description of Reproductions* were developed by CC:DA's Task Force on Multiple Versions and later revised by CC:DA's Task Force to Review the Guidelines for Bibliographic Description of Reproductions. This document, including its section on "Implications of Implementation of the *Guidelines for Bibliographic Description of Reproductions* within the USMARC Format," represents the end-product of five years of intensive research and deliberation. These documents were accepted and endorsed by CC:DA at its Midwinter meetings in February of 1994.

The *Guidelines* were written with the intention that they could be implemented in harmony with AACR2R. They include a definition of what is meant by a *reproduction,* an enumeration of scope, a list of acceptable sources of cataloging data, and also examples of how reproduction cataloging information might be displayed.

Although the *Guidelines* are intended to give catalogers clear guidance in the cataloging decision-making process, the examples are not intended to be prescriptive of a *single,* acceptable method of displaying or organizing reproduction cataloging information. It is anticipated that library system designers will tailor online displays and offline products to meet the needs of their user communities. Furthermore, the "Implications of Implementation . . ." section provides developers with system requirements information that should help them work through implementation issues in computer environments.

As these cataloging guidelines are widely implemented, it is expected that catalogers and system developers will have suggestions for their improvement. In addition, amplifications to address more fully the needs of specialized cataloging communities may be developed by these communities. Any such comments or amplifications should be directed to CC:DA at the following address: American Library Association, Association of Library Collections and Technical Services, Chair, Committee on Cataloging: Description and Access, 50 East Huron Street, Chicago, Illinois 60611.

BRUCE CHR. JOHNSON, *Chair*
CC:DA Task Force to Review the Guidelines for
Bibliographic Description of Reproductions

## Acknowledgments

The Committee on Cataloging: Description and Access gratefully acknowledges the hundreds of written comments and analyses that helped CC:DA to produce these guidelines. A great deal of careful thought went into these written submissions, which in turn allowed the discussion of reproductions cataloging to reach this consensus.

CC:DA also would like to thank the roughly two score members of its two task forces for their hard work and creative thinking. In particular, the following individuals' dedicated service as task force Chair was crucial for the success of this project:

John Attig, Pennsylvania State University

Verna Urbanski, University of North Florida

Jennifer Bowen, Eastman School of Music

Bruce Chr. Johnson, Library of Congress

# GUIDELINES FOR BIBLIOGRAPHIC DESCRIPTION OF REPRODUCTIONS

## I.   Introduction

Inasmuch as the *Anglo-American Cataloguing Rules,* second edition, 1988 revision, with 1993 Amendments (AACR2R) do not adequately provide for the cataloging of reproductions, these guidelines are intended to assist in creating bibliographic descriptions that relate a reproduction to an original. The technique outlined below eliminates the need to *repeat* the description of the original in the description of the reproduction. Instead, the unique features of the reproduction will be recorded separately from the description of the original. Any cataloging element for the reproduction that is identical to the original need not be repeated when cataloging the reproduction.

## II.   Definition of *reproduction*

A reproduction is an item that is a copy of another item and is intended to function as a substitute for that item. The copy may be in a different physical format from the original. Reproduction is a mechanical rather than an intellectual process. Due to the particular mechanical process used to create it, physical characteristics of the reproduction, such as color, image resolution, or sound fidelity may differ from those of the original. Reproductions are usually made for such reasons as the original's limited availability, remote location, poor condition, high cost, or restricted utility.

1

## III. Scope

The reproduction cataloging technique represents an exception to AACR2R; the technique may be applied to reproductions of all types of materials, including reproductions of other reproductions. The following examples are candidates for treatment using the reproduction cataloging technique:

- photocopies
- microform copies
- reprints which are not being considered as distinct editions
- reproductions of full or partial runs of serials and multipart items
- tape dubs of sound recordings and moving image materials
- photomechanical or photographic copies of graphic materials
- computer files produced by optical scanning of a printed original

Do not apply the technique to:

- reprints containing significant intellectual alterations or additions
- simultaneous publications, including US and international editions of printed items where it is impossible to identify the original
- reissues of sound recordings in the same or a different format
- sound or video recordings issued simultaneously in more than one format
- two-dimensional copies of three-dimensional materials
- materials issued simultaneously in print and in electronic formats

Apply this technique to items that the cataloger judges to fit the definition of reproduction and to match the statement of scope. *(See Appendix A for examples.)* If in doubt about whether an item is a reproduction, do not apply this technique. *(See Appendix B for examples.)*

## IV. Bibliographic description of the original

The bibliographic description of the original is prepared by:

A. Utilizing an existing bibliographic description of the original item in the library's catalog; *or*

B. Creating a bibliographic description from:

   1. the original item in hand; *or*

   2. a description of the original found in a reference source (e.g. the *National Union Catalog,* OCLC, RLIN, WLN, UTLAS); *or*

3. the information about the original found in the reproduction; *or*

4. a combination of methods 1–3 above.

When possible, describe the original following the rules in the AACR2R chapter(s) applicable to the type of material constituting the original item. When the bibliographic identity of the original cannot be determined with relative certainty, do not use the reproduction cataloging technique, but rather, catalog the item in hand according to the appropriate AACR2R chapter(s). For reproductions of unique items or collections, such as archives, manuscripts, and visual materials, access to an existing bibliographic description of the original usually will be necessary to establish bibliographic identity.

## V.  Bibliographic description of the reproduction

The bibliographic description of the reproduction contains information specific to the reproduction. Any number of reproductions may be associated with the same original. Describe the reproduction following the rules in the AACR2R chapter(s) applicable to the type of material constituting the reproduction.

The bibliographic description of the reproduction includes only information that varies from the original. Since any cataloging element may be needed, the description of the reproduction may contain any of these elements:

A.  title and/or statement of responsibility information specific to the reproduction

B.  edition statement for the reproduction

C.  material-specific details (if appropriate) for the reproduction

D.  publication, distribution, etc., information for the reproduction

E.  physical description information for the reproduction

F.  series information for the reproduction

G.  notes information for the reproduction

H.  access points specific to the reproduction

If any descriptive data element within an area for the reproduction differs from that of the original and recording only a portion of the area would cause confusion, give the entire area in the bibliographic description of the reproduction. If any aspect or part of the original is lost in the reproduction (e.g., missing pages, loss of color), make a note in the description of the reproduction.

## VI. Relating the description of the reproduction to the description of the original

Display the description of the original before the description of the reproduction. All reproductions, including reproductions of reproductions, should be considered reproductions of the original. Precede the description of the reproduction with a caption containing the word *Reproduction*, the SMD (in its singular form) or another appropriate term (such as *photocopy*) in parentheses, and a colon.

*Examples:*

**Reproduction (photocopy):**

**Reproduction (microfiche):**

**Reproduction (videocassette):**

# EXAMPLES OF REPRODUCTIONS

Unless otherwise indicated, the original items in the following examples are cataloged according to AACR2R and *Library of Congress Rule Interpretations* (LCRI). Some serial examples may not follow CONSER practice; however all follow AACR2R and the LCRI. In an effort to achieve consistency, all data relating to reproduction agencies have been recorded in the publication, distribution, etc. area of reproduction records. This reflects an extension of the LCRI for rule 1.11A ("Non-Microform Preservation Reproductions") to reproductions of all types. All examples of original items represent actual items, although the reproductions in some cases are fictitious. The existence of an example in this Appendix does not constitute a recommendation that the particular type of reproduction shown should necessarily be cataloged. While these examples do not include subject headings, catalogers may wish to include subject headings for originals and/or reproductions. There may be cases under current practice where a reproduction would be assigned a different subject heading from the original, such as those indicating form.

Holdings statements have been added to the examples to show *one possible* method of displaying bibliographic and holdings information together. The holdings statements in Examples 1 through 21 show how this information might appear in the public catalog of a single institution. The holdings statements in Example 22 show how this information might appear in a union catalog showing the holdings of multiple institutions. Examples 2–4 and 8 show one possible method for display when a library owns a reproduction but not the original item. In this situation, some libraries may wish to add a statement such as: "NOT IN LIBRARY'S COLLECTIONS". The holdings statements are constructed according to the NISO standards for holdings statements for serial and nonserial items (Z39.44 and Z39.57), although bracketed captions have been supplied for some examples. As an example of one possible approach to the display of complex serial holdings, composite holdings statements are also provided for serials. Holdings statements for reproductions of serials reflect the enumeration of the original, while those for monographs reflect the enumeration of the reproduction. Compression is utilized when possible and level 3, option A (summary holdings with enumeration and chronology displayed together) is used for serials unless otherwise stated.

1. Microfilm of a text, produced for preservation purposes [original cataloged according to AACR1, Chapter 6 revised]

---

**Abrahams, Harold Maurice, 1899–**
Oxford versus Cambridge : a record of inter-university contests from 1827–1930 / compiled and arranged by H.M. Abrahams . . . and J. Bruce-Kerr . . . — London : Faber and Faber, [1931]
xvii, 619 p. ; 23 cm.
Bibliography: p. [xiii]–xiv.
I. Bruce-Kerr, John.    II. Title.

■ **MAIN — GV693.O9A2**

Reproduction (microfilm): Ann Arbor, Mich. : University Microfilms International, [19--]
1 microfilm reel.
Master microform held by: UnM.

■ **MICROFORMS — Film E94326**

---

2. Published microform reproduction [original not held]

---

**The Siege of Savannah by the combined American and French forces under the command of Gen. Lincoln and the Count D'Estaing in the autumn of 1779.** — Albany : J. Munsell, 1866.
187 p. : port. ; 23 cm.
References: Sabin 33153.

Reproduction (microfiche): Louisville, Ky. : Lost Cause Press, 1975.
3 microfiches : negative.

■ **MICROFORMS — Micro Sabin 33153 — [fiche] 1–3**

---

3.  On-demand macroreproduction

---

**Scillia, Diane Graybowski.**
    Gerard David and manuscript illumination in the Low Countries,
1480–1509 / by Diane Graybowski Scillia. — 1975.
    xvii, 330 leaves, 60 leaves of plates : ill.
    Thesis (Ph. D.) — Case Western Reserve University, 1975.
    Bibliography: leaves 307–330.
    Description based on: Reproduction of 1985.
    I. Title.

Reproduction (photocopy): Ann Arbor, Mich. : University Microfilms
    International, 1985.
    xvii, 330 p., 60 leaves of plates : ill. ; 22 cm.
    "75-27,958" — Half t.p.

■ **MAIN — ND673.D3S3 1985a**

---

4.  Macroreproduction that includes a **different chief source of information;** chief
source for the reproduction is a *data sheet* on the leaf before the reproduced *title
page* of the original

---

**Hoosier National Forest off-road vehicle policy** : USDA Forest Service
    environmental statement / prepared by U.S. Dept. of Agriculture,
    Forest Service, Eastern Region. — [Milwaukee, WI] : The Region,
    1973.
    1 v. (various pagings) : maps ; 28 cm.
    Title from cover.
    Description based on: Reproduction of [1975].
    I. United States. Forest Service. Eastern Region.

Reproduction (photocopy): Off-road vehicle policy, Hoosier National
    Forest : environmental statement. — Springfield, Va. : National Technical
    Information Service, U.S. Dept. of Commerce, [1975]
    1 v. (various pagings) : maps ; 28 cm.
    Title from data sheet.
    "PB-253-641."
    I. Title.

■ **MAIN — SD428.H78U58 1975**

---

5.  Black-and-white microfilm of a book that includes color illustrations

---

**Andree, Richard, 1835–1912.**
     Braunschweiger Volkskunde / von Richard Andree. — 2. verm. Aufl., mit
12 Tafeln und 174 Abbildungen, Plänen und Karten. — Braunschweig :
Vieweg, 1901.
     xviii, 531 p., 12 p. of plates (part col.) : ill., map, 2 ports. ; 24 cm.
     I. Title.

     ■ **MAIN — DD801.B847A5**

Reproduction (microfilm): Cambridge, Mass. : General Microfilm Company,
[19--]
1 microfilm reel ; 35 mm.
Color plates reproduced in black and white.
Master microform held by: GmC.

     ■ **MICROFORMS — Film 2499**

---

6.  Photocopy (printout) of an original microfiche; reproduction agency unknown

---

**Sheahan, Patricia.**
     Geological bibliography of mid-continent basement U.S.A. [microform] /
Patricia Sheahan. —Boulder, Colo. : Geological Society of America, c1984.
     1 microfiche (58 fr.) : negative. — (Microform publication ; 15)
     I. Title.  II. Series.

     ■ **MICROFORMS —Film 9102**

Reproduction (photocopy): [S.l. : s.n., 198-]
     58 leaves ; 28 cm.

     ■ **CORE — QE77.S53 1984a**

---

9.  Photocopy of a map that has been reduced from the size and scale of the original

---

**Illinois. Public Utilities Commission.**
 Railroad map of Illinois, 1916 [map] / prepared under the direction of
State Public Utilities Commission of Illinois. — Scale [1:506,800]. 8 miles
to 1 in. (W 91°45′—W 87°15′/N 42°38′—N 37°00′). — [Springfield, Ill.] :
The Commission, 1916 (Chicago : Rand McNally)
 1 map : col. ; 124 x 79 cm.
 Includes key to steam railroads, list of passenger terminals in Chicago,
and inset of Chicago and vicinity.
 Index of counties and towns on verso.
 I. Rand McNally and Company.   II. Title.

■ **MAPS VAULT — G4101.P3 1916 I38**

Reproduction (photocopy): Scale [ca. 1:1,050,000]. — [Springfield, Ill. :
 Office of Secretary of State, Micrographics Division, 1979]
 1 map ; 61 x 38 cm.

■ **MAPS VAULT — G4101.P3 1916 I38p**

---

10.  Black and white microfiche reproduction of a series of color maps

---

**[Poland]** [map]. — Scale 1:100,000. — Warszaw : Wojskowy Instytut
 Geograficzny, 1922–1935.
 ca. 1,000 maps : col. ; 28 x 37 cm.
 Relief shown by hachures, contours and spot heights.
 I. Wojskowy Instytut Geograficzny (Poland)

■ **MAPS — G6520.S100L5 — ca. 1,000 maps**

Reproduction (microfiche): [Santa Cruz, Calif. : Western Association of Map
 Libraries, 1988]
 1,253 microfiches.
 Includes multiple editions of some sheets.
 Color maps reproduced in black and white.

■ **MAPS MICROFORMS — Fiche US2928 — Fiche 1–226,Fiche
 230–967,Fiche 969–1253**

---

11. Microform copy of an archival collection of personal papers (*[etc.]* indicates portions of record here omitted for the sake of brevity) [original cataloged according to Hensen's *Archives, personal papers, and manuscripts*]

---

**Oppen, George.**
Papers, 1958–1984.
14.2 cu. ft. (34 boxes).
Arranged in 9 series: 1. Correspondence. 2. Notes, jottings, etc.
3. Daybooks. 4. Poetry. *[etc.]*
Objectivist poet, winner of the Pulitzer Prize in 1969. Born in 1908 in New Rochelle, New York. Married Mary Colby in 1927. *[etc.]*
Summary: Includes manuscripts and typescripts for all 9 of Oppen's published volumes of poetry; ca. 300 unpublished poems; extensive personal notes and daybooks; typescripts of essays; and transcriptions of interviews. *[etc.]*
Restrictions: Access to originals is restricted; readers must use microfilm.
Cite as: George Oppen papers. MSS 16. University Library, Mandeville Dept. of Special Collections, University of California, San Diego.
Literary rights retained by Linda Oppen Mourelatos.
Acquired 1984, 1986.
Unpublished finding aid available in the library: folder level control.
I. Title: George Oppen papers.

■ **MANUSCRIPTS AND ARCHIVES — MSS 16 — 34 boxes**

Reproduction (microfilm): Los Angeles, Calif. : Filmed by University of California Reprographic Services for the University of California, San Diego, 1988.
33 microfilm reels ; 35 mm.

■ **MICROFORMS — Film 10357 — Reel 1–33**

---

12. Microfilm copy of a piece of music

---

**Danzi, Margarethe, 1768–1800.**
[Sonatas, violin, piano, op. 1]
Trois sonates pour le piano forte avec violon oblige, oeuvre I / composée
par Madame Danzi née Marchand. — Munic [sic] : chez Mac Falter, [17--?]
2 parts ; 33 cm.
References: RISM A/I, D 1045.

■ **RARE BOOKS — M219.D199 op.1 1700z — 2 parts**

Reproduction (microfilm): München : Bayerische Staatsbibliothek, 1982.
1 microfilm reel ; 35 mm.

■ **MICROFORMS — Microfilm 2275**

---

13. Tape dub of a 33 1/3 rpm sound recording [original cataloged according to
AACR1, Chapter 14 revised]

---

**Mahler, Gustav, 1860–1911.**
[Symphonies, no. 2, C minor] [Sound recording]
Symphony no. 2, in C minor (Resurrection) Columbia M2L–256. [1958]
2 discs. 33 1/3 rpm. 12 in. (Columbia masterworks)
New York Philharmonic; Emilia Cundari, soprano; Maureen Forrester,
contralto; Westminster Choir; Bruno Walter, conductor.
In container; automatic sequence.
Program notes by Bruno Walter and texts of the vocal portion, with
English translation, on outer slipcase.
I. New York Philharmonic. II. Cundari, Emilia. III. Forrester,
Maureen. IV. Walter, Bruno, 1876–1962. V. Westminster Choir.

■ **LISTENING CENTER — LP 256 — Disc 1–2**

Reproduction (sound tape): Rochester, N.Y. : Sibley Music Library, Eastman
School of Music, 1991.
1 sound tape reel : analog, 7 1/2 ips, 2 tracks, mono. ; 12 in.
Accompanied by photocopy of program notes.

■ **LISTENING CENTER — Tape 65**

---

14.  Video reproduction of a 35 mm film reproduced for preservation purposes (*[etc.]* indicates portions of record here omitted for the sake of brevity)

---

**She wore a yellow ribbon** [motion picture] / RKO ; producers, John Ford, Merian C. Cooper ; associate producer, Lowell Farrell ; director, John Ford ; screenplay, Frank Nugent, Laurence Stallings. — United States : RKO, c1949.
  6 film reels (103 min.) : sd., col. ; 35 mm.
  Author, James Warner Bellah.
  Cast: John Wayne, Joanne Dru, John Agar, Ben Johnson, Harry Carey, Jr., Victor McLaglen, Mildred Natwick, George O'Brien, Arthur Shields, Harry Woods, Chief Big Tree, Noble Johnson, Cliff Lyons, Tom Tyler, Michael Dugan, Mickey Simpson, Frank McGrath, Don Summer, Fred Libbey, Jack Pennick, Billy Jones, Bill Goettinger, Fred Graham, Fred Kennedy, Rudy Bowman, Post Parks, Ray Hyke, Lee Bradley.
  Credits: Art director, James Basevi; musical director, C. Bakaleinikoff; photography, Winton Hoch; editor, Jack Murray.
  All credits were supplied from: Film daily yearbook, 1950.
  Safety film base; optical sound; filmed using the 3-color Technicolor process; Eastmancolor print.
  Original running time was 103 min., according to: Film daily yearbook, 1950.
  I. Ford, John, 1894–1973.   II. Cooper, Merian C.   III. Nugent, Frank.
IV. Stallings, Laurence, 1894–1968.   V. Wayne, John, 1907–1979.
VI. Dru, Joanne, 1923–     VII. Agar, John, 1921– *[etc.]*

■ **FILM ARCHIVES — MP 619 — Reel 1–6**

Reproduction (videocassette): [Los Angeles, Ca. : Taped by UCLA Film and Television Archives, 1988]
  1 videocassette (103 min.) : sd., col. ; 1/2 in.
  VHS.

■ **AUDIOVISUAL — VC 201**

---

15. Photoreproduction of a graphic item [original cataloged according to Betz's *Graphic materials*]

---

**Rembrandt Harmenszoon van Rijn, 1606–1669.**
[The three trees] [graphic] / [Rembrandt Harmenszoon van Rijn]. —
[1643]
   1 print : etching ; image 20 x 28 cm.
   Image trimmed to or within plate mark at bottom.
   References: Biorklund, 43-B; Rovinskii, 212.
   Gift of Mrs. Gardiner Greene Hubbard, 1898.
   I. Title.

   ■ **PRINTS AND PHOTOGRAPHS READING ROOM —
    Print 73–104**

Reproduction (transparency): [Washington, D.C. : Library of Congress
   Photoduplication Service, 1988]
   1 transparency : Kodacolor ; 35 mm.

   ■ **PRINTS AND PHOTOGRAPHS READING ROOM —
    Slide 88–411**

---

16. Copy negative and microreproduction of an original photographic negative [original cataloged according to Betz's *Graphic materials*]

---

**Barnard, George N., 1819–1902, photographer.**
   [Centreville, Va., stone church] [graphic]. — 1862 March.
   1 negative : glass, wet collodion ; 8 x 10 in.
   I. Title.

   ■ **PRINTS AND PHOTOGRAPHS READING ROOM —**
   **Slide 88–4551**

Reproduction (negative): [Washington, D.C. : Library of Congress
   Photoduplication Service, 1961]
   1 negative : film ; 8 x 10 in.

   ■ **PRINTS AND PHOTOGRAPHS READING ROOM —**
   **Negative 88–4551a**

Reproduction (microfilm): [Washington, D.C. : Library of Congress
   Photoduplication Service, 1980]
   1 microfilm frame ; 35 mm.

   ■ **MICROFORM READING ROOM — Reel 80–128**

---

17. Remote access computer file, reproduced on disks

---

**Geoecology data base** [computer file] / Ronald W. Matheny, program manager. — Computer data. — Oak Ridge, Tenn. : Oak Ridge National Laboratory, [1981?]
Title from guide.
"ORNL/TM-7351."
Accompanied by guide: Geoecology, a county-level environmental data base for the coterminous United States / R.C. Olson, C.J. Emerson, and M.K. Nungesser. — (Environmental Sciences Division publication ; no. 1537).
"Contains selected data on terrain and soils, water resources, forestry, vegetation, agriculture, land use, wildlife, air quality, climate, natural areas, and endangered species. Basic files on human population are also included to complement the environmental files" — Guide abstract.
Bibliography: p. 43–54 of guide.
I. Matheny, Ronald W.    II. Olson, R. J. (Richard J.)    III. Emerson, C. J. IV. Nungesser, Martha K.    V. Title: Geoecology.    VI. Series: Environmental Sciences Division publication ; no. 1537.

■ **For access to this file, inquire at the Reference Desk**

Reproduction (computer disk): [Ithaca, N.Y. : Mann Library, Cornell University, 1988]
10 disks ; 5 1/4 in. + 1 guide.
Guide is a photocopy of the original.

■ **MICROCOMPUTER CENTER — QH104.G34 1981a —**
**Disk 1–10  + 1 guide**

---

18.  Microreproductions of a current serial

---

**The Serials librarian.** — Vol. 1, no. 1 (fall 1976)–   . — [New York, NY :
Haworth Press, 1976–   ]
   v. ; 26 cm.
Quarterly.
Title from cover.
Has supplement: Monographic supplement to the Serials librarian.
Published: New York, NY, 1976–      ; Binghamton, NY,
ISSN 0361-526X = The Serials librarian.

■ **Composite holdings: v.1 (1976)–**

■ **PERIODICALS**[1] **— v.17:no.1 (1992:winter)–v.17:no.2
(1992:spring); Retained until microfilm is received**

Reproduction (microfiche): Ann Arbor, Mich. : University Microfilms
International, [1976?–   ]
   microfiches.

■ **MICROFORMS — Micro Per S48 — v.2 (1977)–v.4 (1979),v.7
(1982)–v.10 (1986)**

Reproduction (microfilm): Dayton, Ohio : NCR Information Imaging
Systems, [197-?–   ]
   microfilm reels.

■ **MICROFORMS — Microfilm Per S48 — v.1 (1976)–**

---

1. This holdings statement is constructed at level 4.

19. Reproductions of a serial which has ceased publication. The original was cataloged according to AACR1 with ISBD punctuation added

---

**The American museum, or, Universal magazine.** — Vol. 7, no. 1 (Jan. 1790)–v. 10, no. 6 (Dec. 1791); pt. 1 (Jan.–June 1792)–pt. 2 (July–Dec. 1792). — [Philadelphia, Pa. : Carey, Stewart, and Co.], 1790–1792.
6 v. : ill., map ; 23 cm.
Monthly.
Title from masthead.
Subtitle: Containing essays on agriculture, commerce, manufactures, politics, morals and manners; sketches of national characters, natural and civil history, and biography; law information, public papers, intelligence; moral tales, ancient and modern poetry.
Editor: M. Carey.
Continues: American magazine.
I. Carey, Mathew, 1760–1839.   II. Title: American museum.   III. Title: Universal magazine.

■ **Composite holdings: v.7 (1790)–v.10 (1791) pt.1 (1792)–pt.2 (1792)**

■ **RARE BOOKS — AP2.A2A8 — v. 7 no. 3 (Mar. 1790)**

Reproduction (microfiche): Louisville, [Ky.] : Lost Cause Press, 1966.
66 microfiches : negative, ill., map. — (Selected Americana from Sabin's Dictionary of books relating to America, from its discovery to the present time) (Fichebook)
I. Series: Selected Americana from Sabin's Dictionary of books relating to America, from its discovery to the present time.   II. Series: Fichebook.

■ **MICROFORMS — Micro SELAMER A545 — v.7 (1790)–v.10 (1791); pt.1 (1792)–pt.2 (1792)**

Reproduction (microfilm): Ann Arbor, Mich. : University Microfilms, 1942.
on 1 microfilm reel : ill., map ; 35 mm. — (American periodical series, 18th century ; 5)
Some pages missing.
I. Series.

■ **MICROFORMS — Microfilm APS18 no. 5 — v.7 (1790)–v.10 (1791), pt.1 (1792)–pt.2 (1792)**

Reproduction (microopaque): Louisville, [Ky.] : Lost Cause Press, 1966.
on 75 of 148 microopaques : ill., map ; 8 x 13 cm. — (Selected Americana from Sabin's Bibliotheca Americana)
I. Series: Selected Americana from Sabin's Dictionary of books relating to America, from its discovery to the present time.

■ **MICROFORMS — Micro SELAMER A545 — v.7 (1790)–v.10 (1791), pt.1 (1792)–pt.2 (1792)**

20.  Microfiche reproduction with a variant title on the fiche header

---

**PCI journal** / Prestressed Concrete Institute. — Vol. 20, no. 1 (Jan./Feb.
1975)–    . — Chicago, Ill. : The Institute, 1975–
    v. : ill. ; 23 cm.
Bimonthly.
Title from cover.
Other title: Prestressed Concrete Institute journal.
Continues: Journal of the Prestressed Concrete Institute.
Issued by: Precast/Prestressed Concrete Institute, Mar./Apr. 1989–    .
ISSN 0887-9672 = PCI journal.
    I. Prestressed Concrete Institute.    II. Precast/Prestressed Concrete
Institute.    III. Title: Prestressed Concrete Institute journal.

■ **Composite holdings: v.20 (1975) –**

■ **PERIODICALS — TA680.P83 — Retained until microfilm is
received**

Reproduction (microfiche): Ann Arbor, Mich. : University Microfilms
    International, [19-- –    ]
        microfiches.
Title on fiche header: Precast/Prestressed Concrete Institute journal.
    I. Title: Precast/Prestressed Concrete Institute journal.

■ **MICROFORM READING ROOM — TA680.P83a — v.20 (1975) –**

---

21. Printout of a serial issued electronically

---

**Newsletter on serials pricing issues** [computer file]. — Computer data. —
No. 2 (Mar. 30, 1989) –   . — [Chicago, Ill. : s.n., 1989 –   ]
Mode of access: subscription through BITNET or ALANET.
Irregular.
Title from caption.
No. 4 has title: Newsletter on serials pricing.
Continues: ALA/RTSD newsletter on serials pricing issues.
No. 2– published by the Resources and Technical Services Division of
the American Library Association; no. – published by the Division under its
later name: Association for Library Collections and Technical Services; no. –
published by the editor.
Also available on DATALINX; issued also on paper.
ISSN 1046-3410 = Newsletter on serials pricing issues.
I. American Library Association. Resources and Technical Services
Division.    II. Association for Library Collections & Technical Services.
III. Title: Newsletter on serials pricing.

■ **Composite holdings: no.2 (1989) –**

■ **Available on library's local area network; inquire at Reference
Desk for assistance.**

Reproduction (printout): [Berkeley, Ca. : Printed out by School of Library
and Information Science, University of California, Berkeley, 198- –   ]
v. ; 28 cm.

■ **PERIODICALS — Z683.N28a — no.2 (1989) –**

---

22.  Complex serial reproduction, including reproductions of partial runs with mixed
paper and microform holdings

**Federal register.** — Washington, D.C. : Office of the Federal Register,
National Archives and Records Service, General Services Administration :
Supt. of Docs., U.S. G.P.O., [distributor],
v. ; 28 cm.
Daily (except Saturday, Sunday, and official Federal holidays)
Began with Vol. 1, no. 1 (Mar. 14, 1936).
Mar. 14, 1936–Mar. 23, 1951 issued by the Division of the Federal
Register; Mar. 24, 1951–Mar. 25, 1959 by the Federal Register Division;
Mar. 26, 1959–Mar. 29, 1985 by the Office of the Federal Register, National
Archives and Records Service, General Services Administration; Apr. 1,
1985– by the Office of the Federal Register, National Archives and Records
Administration.
Vols. for      distributed to some depository libraries in microfiche.
Issued also on compact disc; also available through the LEXIS system.
Includes annual index; some issues have additional pts. on special subjects.
Description based on: Vol. 49, no. 1 (Jan. 3, 1984); title from cover.
ISSN 0097-6326 = Federal register.
I. United States. Division of the Federal Register.     II. United States.
Federal Register Division.     III. United States. Office of the Federal
Register.

■ **Network composite holdings: v.1 (1936) –**

■ **Network holdings in this format: v.1 (1936) –**

  ■ **Composite holdings:**

| | |
|---|---|
| CLobS | v.1 (1936) – |
| GGS | v.14 (1949) – |
| LRuL | v.1 (1936) – |
| NAILS | v.1 (1936) – |
| NIC | v.1 (1936) – |
| NbChS | v.1 (1936) –v.52 (1988) |

  ■ **Holdings:**

| | |
|---|---|
| CLobS | Per KF70.A2 — v.30 (1965) – |
| GGS | READING ROOM — Last 12 months only |
| NAILS | c.1: US Ref KF70.A2 — v.1 (1936) – |
| | c.2: STACKS — KF70.A2 — v.1 (1936) – |
| NIC | LAW — Ref KF 70 A2 — v.1 (1936) – |
| | MANN — KF 70 A2 F29 — v.1 (1936) – |
| | OLIN — Gov Docs GS 4.107 — v.1 (1936) – |
| | URIS — Per — Last 10 years only |
| NbChS | KF70.A2 — v.1 (1936) –v.52 (1988) |

*[continued]*

*[Example 22 continued]*

Reproduction (microfiche): Washington, D.C. : Capitol Services, [19-- –   ]
   microfiches.

■ **Holdings:**
| | |
|---|---|
| NAlLS | **MICROFICHE — KF70.A2 — v.1 (1936) –** |
| NIC | **LAW — Microform F2428 — v.1 (1936) –** |

Reproduction (microfiche): Washington, D.C. : Congressional Information
   Service, [19-- –   ]
   microfiches : negative.

■ **Holdings:**
| | |
|---|---|
| NbChS | **MICROFORM READING ROOM — v.17 (1952) –v.42 (1977)** |

Reproduction (microfiche): Englewood, Colo. : Information Handling
   Services, [19-- –   ]
   microfiches : negative.

■ **Holdings:**
| | |
|---|---|
| CLobS | **SPEC MAT — MC S00327 — v.1 (1936) –v.29 (1964)** |
| NIC | **MANN — Fiche 3190 — v.18 (1953) –** |

Reproduction (microfiche): Ann Arbor, Mich. : University Microfilms,
   [19-- –   ]
   microfiches.

■ **Holdings:**
| | |
|---|---|
| GGS | **Fiche F214 — v.40 (1975) –** |

Reproduction (microfiche): [S.l. : NCR?, 1976?–   ]
   microfiches : negative ; 8 x 13 cm.
   Header: U.S. Nat. Arch. Fed. Reg.
   I. United States. National Archives. II. Title: U.S. Nat. Arch. Fed. reg.

■ **Holdings:**
| | |
|---|---|
| NIC | **URIS — Ref Fiche 516 — v.41 (1976) –** |

Reproduction (microfiche): 1980–   . — Buffalo, N.Y. : Hein, 1983–
   microfiches : negative.
   Issued with: List of CFR sections affected.

■ **Holdings:**
| | |
|---|---|
| LRuL | **MICROFORMS — Fiche 80063 — v.45 (1980) –** |

*[continued]*

*[Example 22 continued]*

Reproduction (microfilm): Princeton, N.J. : Princeton Microfilm Corp.,
    [19-- –   ]
        microfilm reels : negative ; 35 mm.

■ **Holdings:**
    **GGS**              **Film F118 — v.14 (1949) –v.39 (1974)**

Reproduction (microfilm): Ann Arbor, Mich. : University Microfilms
    International, [19-- –   ]
        microfilm reels ; 35 mm.
    Issued with: Federal register index and List of CFR sections affected (Jan.
    1972–Feb. 1975), Cumulative list of CFR sections affected (Mar. 1975 –June
    1977), LSA, list of CFR sections affected (July 1977–   ).

■ **Holdings:**
    **LRuL**             **MICROFORMS — Film 733 — v.1 (1936) –v.48**
                         **(1983)**
    **NIC**              **OLIN — MMN Film 1784 — v.1 (1936) –**

Reproduction (microfilm): Washington : National Archives, National
    Archives and Records Service, General Services Administration, 1950–
        microfilm reels ; 35 mm. — (National Archives microfilm
    publications)
        Published daily, Tuesday through Saturday (not published on day after an
    official holiday)
        I. Series.

■ **Holdings:**
    **NAILS**            **Microfilm KF 70 A2 — v.1 (1936) –**

Reproduction (microopaque): [Washington, D.C.? : Micro Card, 1954?–   ]
        microopaques ; 8 x 13 cm.
        Header: U.S. Nat. Arch. Fed. Reg.
        I. United States. National Archives. II. Title: U.S. Nat. Arch. Fed. reg.

■ **Holdings:**
    **NIC**              **OLIN — MMN Card 96 — v.1 (1936) –v.35 (1970)**

Reproduction (microopaque): [S.l.] : NCR, [1968?–   ]
        microopaques ; 8 x 13 cm.
        Header: U.S. Nat. Arch. Fed. Reg.
        I. United States. National Archives. II. Title: U.S. Nat. Arch. Fed. reg.

■ **Holdings:**
    **NIC**              **OLIN — MMN Card 96 — v.35 (1970) –v.41 (1977)**

# EXAMPLES OF ITEMS THAT ARE NOT TO BE TREATED AS REPRODUCTIONS

1. Hardcover and paperback issues of the same book with no significant bibliographic differences

   *Describe as two copies of a single edition.*

2. A monograph simultaneously issued in the United States and the United Kingdom by two different publishers

   *Describe as distinct editions; neither can be identified as the original.*

3. A book issued both in conventional-sized type and large print

   *Describe as distinct editions.*

4. A Braille edition of a book

   *Describe as a distinct edition; a Braille version is not simply a mechanical copy of the original.*

5. An annotated version of a novel

   *Describe as a distinct edition; contains significant intellectual additions.*

6. Published music, whether full-size or reduced, that appears to have been printed from the same metal or photographic plates as an earlier edition

   *Describe as distinct editions, unless the later publication is clearly identified as a reproduction of the earlier one.*

7. A microfilm of a manuscript collection which contains significant omissions, additions, or alterations from the original

   *Describe as distinct editions.*

8.  A microfilm consisting of manuscript scores collected from various sources

    *Describe the microfilm collection as an original microfilm, since it is the first appearance of these scores* **as a collection.** *The individual works in the collection, however, may be described as reproductions of the individual manuscript scores.*

9.  A full score and a set of parts for a string quartet

    *Describe as distinct editions or as a single edition, depending upon how the items are published; the two types do not serve as substitutes for each other.*

10. A sound recording issued on LP, CD, and cassette

    *Describe as distinct editions; it is difficult to determine (1) which is the original, and (2) that the others are exact copies.*

11. An LP issued in both monaural and stereo

    *Describe as distinct editions; neither can be identified as the original.*

12. An LP reissued as a CD

    *Describe as a distinct edition; it is difficult to determine that it is an exact copy; its creation probably involved both mechanical and intellectual processes.*

13. A computer application package issued on both 3 1/2- and 5 1/4-inch disks

    *Describe as distinct editions or treat as copies of a single edition; neither can be identified as the original.*

14. A computerized version of an encyclopedia originally published in paper form with search software added

    *Describe as a distinct edition; the computerized version contains additional features not present in the printed encyclopedia.*

15. A journal published simultaneously in printed and electronic formats

    *Describe as distinct editions; neither can be identified as the original.*

16. A museum reproduction of an art original

    *Describe as distinct editions unless it can be verified that the reproduction is an exact copy of the original.*

17. A video issued in both Beta and VHS

    *Describe as distinct editions; neither can be identified as the original.*

# IMPLICATIONS OF IMPLEMENTATION OF THE *GUIDELINES FOR BIBLIOGRAPHIC DESCRIPTION OF REPRODUCTIONS* WITHIN THE USMARC FORMAT

## Background

The Committee on Cataloging: Description and Access (CC:DA) has developed guidelines for describing multiple versions and making recommendations about changes to AACR2R, if needed.

The starting point for the CC:DA's discussions was the description of the two-tier hierarchical model contained in the *Multiple Versions Forum Report.* In this model, the hierarchy consists of an independent bibliographic record for the original and dependent holdings records for reproductions linked to the bibliographic record for the original. This two-tier model is meant to provide catalogers with a practical means for communicating bibliographic information for materials that are viewed as reproductions. Eventually the model might be found to be applicable to other materials as well.

Following the two-tier model recommended in the *Multiple Versions Forum Report,* we have a primary bibliographic description and a bibliographic description subordinated within a holdings record. This mixing of holdings and bibliographic information is problematic. It obscures bibliographic relationships; it also makes the maintenance of shared bibliographic information difficult in a multi-institutional database.

## Bibliographic considerations

While pre-AACR2 dashed-on cataloging of reproductions was a quick, useful tool for bringing reproductions under a minimal level of control, it was never adequate for meaningfully recording reproduction-specific cataloging information. Imprint and collation information could be recorded, but variations of title, edition, series, and subject headings were treated much less precisely (if at all). Indeed, much reproduction cataloging was (and still is) done by compromise and expediency. An example of this is the coding conventions for recording fixed field-type information for the reproduction in a MARC record. Field 008 data elements are set for the original; field 533 subfield ǂ7 for the reproduction. There is no easy way to record differences in title, edition, and subject heading. It would be preferable for all data to be recorded, coded, searched, and retrieved the same way, regardless of whether the data describes an original or a reproduction.

*Guidelines for Bibliographic Description of Reproductions* addresses the problem of cataloging reproductions by defining what is meant by the term reproduction and spelling out how reproductions of any distribution medium should be described. For example, after evaluating the extent of the problem, CC:DA concluded that the challenge of describing the reproduction of a computer file had much in common with describing the reproduction of a book. In addition, CC:DA decided that providing bibliographic description and access to reproductions requires the same level of completeness as is expected for originals.

From a cataloging perspective, a primary issue is the relationship of descriptions for an original and a reproduction. The two items can be represented:

- in the same description, as in the U.S. Newspaper Project;

- in totally distinct descriptions, in which the description for the reproduction emphasizes either the original (as does the *Library of Congress Rule Interpretations* [LCRI] for microreproductions and on-demand macroreproductions), or the reproduction (as does AACR2R **as written**);

- in a hierarchical fashion, as described in the *Guidelines*, in which the original is represented by its description and the reproduction is represented by the description for the original with an additional, dependent, nonredundant description pertaining specifically to the reproduction.

Clearly, the primary ways in which this relationship will affect end users are display and access. Will they see a single large record, two records in which all or most of the first is duplicated in the second, or a main record and a subordinate, nonredundant record? Where will holdings appear in relation to bibliographic data? All reproduction-specific access points need to be searchable.

## Communications considerations

Decisions regarding the structure and organization of cataloging descriptions affect the structure and organization of USMARC records, but do not fully dictate them. It is important to examine the impact the former have on the latter in order to understand the full range of options available to us. The implication for USMARC of the above bibliographic considerations is that, however the data is stored, the appropriate form of display must be reconstructible and access points must be easily and correctly indexable.

One issue is, how many records to use for an original and a reproduction. Bibliographic information can be stored/communicated:

- **In one record:** All bibliographic data for a reproduction are stored in a single record. If an original and a reproduction are to be displayed as a single description, the data applicable to the original should receive normal content designation. Information that is applicable only to the reproduction is stored in one of two methods: either in a single field which contains necessarily limited content designation (*viz.* 533); or in a fully content-designated way analogous to the 886 field for foreign MARC data. If an original and a reproduction are to be displayed as distinct descriptions, either of these two methods could be used. (Of course, if the LCRI for Chapter 11 of AACR2R were not to be followed, the placement of data related to the original and the reproduction would be switched in both of the methods.)

- **In two records:** Bibliographic data applicable to the original are stored in one record, while bibliographic data applicable only to the reproduction are stored in a subordinate record.

- **In two records:** Bibliographic data applicable to the original are stored in one record, while all bibliographic data applicable to the reproduction are stored in a separate, independent record (as described in AACR2R).

The *Multiple Versions Forum Report* recommended that bibliographic data for the reproduction be stored in holdings records using the two-tier model.

While this approach is one model for USMARC records in a communications environment, it oversimplifies the bibliographic relationships involved. Specifically, using the holdings format for the reproduction's record results in one record with two quite distinct types of information:

- descriptive information about the reproduction regardless of its physical location

- location and holdings information about the reproduction for a particular institution

Holdings data could either be stored in the same records as bibliographic data (for simple situations), or as a separate record. While there is no reason why these two types of information cannot be communicated together in the same "holdings' record, there are functional distinctions about how the two types of information are used that need to be supported by systems dealing with reproduction records. In addition, the user community has traditionally seen bibliographic data as static, while holdings data are seen as fluid. This has been a fundamental consideration for keeping bibliographic and holdings information separate.

Within an institution's catalog there will be cases in which the same reproduction is held at different locations. There will also be cases in which the holdings in those different locations may vary (for example, a complete copy in the main library, only the last three years in the science library). To avoid duplication of information and effort, the database should contain only one descriptive record for each reproduction.

Among the criteria proposed in the *Multiple Versions Forum Report* for evaluating communications techniques were "effective end user access," "effective library staff use," "efficient creation and maintenance of records," and "cost effectiveness." Effective access for users requires a reduction of duplicate information and an organized layout of information display. Effective and efficient record creation and maintenance has the same requirements as effective shared cataloging: one-time cataloging of each reproduction. This means that in resource databases (e.g., OCLC, RLIN) only one descriptive record for each reproduction should appear. Once that record is created, it should be used by all institutions.

## Union database considerations

The type of information hitherto communicated by the *USMARC Format for Holdings Data* traditionally applies to items in individual institutions. Functionally, any union database (which includes holdings information about more than one institution) will need to maintain separate holdings information for each institution. In contrast, the bibliographic information about the reproduction will be the same for all copies of a particular reproduction. Many institutions may hold copies of the same commercially produced reproduction. The bibliographic information about each version represents that unique item in the same sense that the bibliographic information about an edition of a work represents that unique edition; one description applies to, and can be used for, all copies. Thus any union database need include only one description of a particular reproduction. This can save the time of technical processing staff and allow more readable displays for users.

When communicating information about reproductions from the cataloging institution to a shared, union catalog, it may be necessary to use multiple holdings records. This would be true when holdings differ between locations. From the point of view of a union database, there would certainly be cases in which records for the same reproduction are received from several institutions. As these records are incorporated into the database, it would be necessary for different types of data in holdings records to be handled differently. The location and holdings for each institution will need to be maintained. The bibliographic description of the reproduction, however, will need to be compared with other such descriptions in the database.

Descriptions of the same reproduction will have to be matched and either merged or clustered. This task implies either a considerable investment in manual database maintenance or the development of an extremely sophisticated machine-matching algorithm. The former alternative is costly and inefficient. The latter alternative is difficult and highly prone to false matches and nonmatches.

The reason why matching on the data in a reproduction record in the holdings format is so difficult is that the data in the reproduction record are not particularly suited for matching. Given that all information that also applies to the original is omitted, what is left is primarily (1) the type of reproduction, which is given in parentheses following the caption *Reproduction* and in the physical description; (2) publication, etc., information, including dates of publication; (3) series information, if applicable; and (4) notes. None of these is well suited for matching.

1. It would not be too difficult to distinguish a microform reproduction from a computer file reproduction. It would not even be too difficult to distinguish a microfilm from a microfiche. But it might also be necessary to distinguish positive from negative microforms, masters from service copies, etc.

2. The most distinctive matching element in the record is probably the date, but too many reproductions are not explicitly dated. Matching on inferred or incomplete dates is problematic. If more than one reproduction could be published in the same year, it would be necessary to match on the publisher. Unfortunately, the rules for recording publisher information allow a fair degree of latitude in deciding exactly how to record the publisher's name. This makes machine matching unreliable.

3. Series matching, particularly if the items are numbered, might be the more reliable match. However, not all reproductions are in series, and not all series are numbered.

4. The notes might well contain information needed for identification, particularly notes on the physical description. However, finding this information and using it for matching purposes would be extremely difficult.

In summary, although records can be communicated using the two-tier model, it may not be efficient. Different parts of the reproduction record need to be processed in different ways. Other communications models should be examined. Given a careful investigation of user needs, it is our belief that a three-tier model will still need to be employed for managing union databases and for displaying information about reproductions to catalog users, even if a two-tier model is used for communication. Converting two-tier communications records to three-tier database structures seems to us to present significant difficulties that will have to be overcome in union databases.

## Conclusion

Bibliographic and holdings data related to a reproduction need to be processed differently since the two types of data have different uses. Communicating such information in a single holdings record makes efficient data processing difficult.

A more effective model uses a full bibliographic description for the original with dependent bibliographic descriptions for each reproduction of the original with holdings records subordinate to each applicable bibliographic record. This scheme relates holdings directly to either the bibliographic description of the original or to the bibliographic description for one of the reproductions. Keeping in mind that the bibliographic description for the reproduction would contain only information that varies from the original (unique description and access), some savings of cataloging effort should occur since multiple users would be able to use an existing original record and attach a brief reproduction record or use an existing reproduction record and merely attach their holdings.